*To Sarah, Mabli & Tamsin*
*who made it possible for me to tell my story.*

Paul Whittaker

# GODS & KINGS

OBERON BOOKS
LONDON

WWW.OBERONBOOKS.COM

First published in 2019 by Oberon Books Ltd
521 Caledonian Road, London N7 9RH
Tel: +44 (0) 20 7607 3637 / Fax: +44 (0) 20 7607 3629
e-mail: info@oberonbooks.com
www.oberonbooks.com

PB ISBN: 9781786827784
E ISBN: 9781786827791

Cover image: John Campbell / roomoflight.com

Text and layout design by Konstantinos Vasdekis

10 9 8 7 6 5 4 3 2 1

# Contents

# A word from the writer

*Gods & Kings* is the story of how, as a twenty-three-year-old Film Student, I was diagnosed with bipolar manic depression. But it is not just a bracingly honest autobiographical story about mental illness. It is also a show about identity.

This is crucial to the success of the play, as it allows people to connect with the central character even if they have no understanding of bipolar, or have no experience of mental illness. They can still empathise with the character's dilemma because, throughout our lives, we have all had those moments where we question our identity and our purpose. And that opens the story up to a whole variety of conversations.

At points this story is excruciatingly uncomfortable for me to share, but on deciding to share my personal life in this way, I knew the best way to make it mean something was to keep it authentic. There are moments from my life that I still can't watch when they are portrayed on the stage. They will always be part of me, but I know the value in sharing them from the comments that people have made after seeing it. And it's the brutal honesty that people truly connect to.

It was over two decades between being diagnosed and writing the play. As I will always be a service user, I made the decision to write the play in direct address from the service user's point of view, so the audience can experience the world as I saw it, and still do. So every time I faced an editorial decision, I put myself in the audience, with the knowledge that once upon a time I was a person lost in their mental health journey, who would have been attracted to see this work. And so I just kept asking myself the question: "If I was sitting in the dark, surrounded by strangers, would this feel real? Would this feel authentic?"

All too often I've had the experience of sitting in a theatre, or watching a film or a television drama, or listening to the radio, and because the writer has used mental illness as a device for the narrative, or as an intriguing character trait, there is a point where it becomes inconsistent and jarring to me. It makes me angry that someone hadn't taken the time to research and portray a condition authentically, because there is already enough misinformation out there, fuelling misunderstandings that I face every day of my life. I knew that even if a moment was painful and shameful, if it was honest, it needed to stay true – because that is the only way that people are going to really learn what it's like to live with a chronic mental illness.

Because I'd had an undiagnosed mental illness all my life at the time of my diagnosis, I didn't know which parts of me were symptoms, and which were my personality traits. So when I left the psychiatrist's office with the life-changing decision of, "Do I take the lithium, or don't I take the lithium?" I asked myself two crucial questions: "What parts of me are me, and what parts of me are my mental illness?" and: "If I took the lithium, what parts of me would remain and what parts would I lose?" I was under the illusion that lithium would take away my symptoms, and with it, parts of my personality.

I didn't know who would be left, once the drugs separated the condition from who I was. So that's the dilemma at the heart of the play. And that's the issue that people even without mental illness can relate to. When does taking away an illness or a condition start taking away the person as well?

# The Production

*Gods & Kings* was first performed at Sherman Theatre on 6th September 2017.

### Writer / Co-Director / Producer – Paul Whittaker
Paul is a Cardiff-based artist, writer and filmmaker. Having worked as a freelance filmmaker for over a decade, Paul completed his Masters in Creative Writing at Swansea University, achieving the grade of distinction. Paul has exhibited as a digital artist, and worked in theatre, television, dance and independent film. As well as creating his own work he has worked with many clients including Rubicon Dance, Arts Council Wales, Sherman Theatre, Channel 4, Public Health Wales and the Old Vic. His work has been screened on television, at festivals, in art galleries and theatres. His work for Public Health Wales has been viewed both nationally and internationally online.

### Co-Director / Sound / Movement – Tamsin Griffiths
Tamsin Griffiths is a bilingual multimedia artist and performer who works in theatre, film, sound & visual arts to create topical work that questions and challenges perceptions, particularly around the subject of mental health. Tamsin has worked bilingually on a national and international scale in both the arts and health sectors, using her skills, knowledge and experiences within the two to bridge the gap. Tamsin has worked with many organisations, including: Arts Council Wales, Public Health Wales, British Council for Wales, National Assembly for Wales, National Centre for Mental Health, Cardiff University School of Medicine, Cardiff University, Disability Arts Cymru.

### Actor – Robert Bowman
Robert is an actor, teacher and director. He is co-director of Living Pictures. He has worked with the RSC, RNT, Royal Court, Young Vic, Globe, Sherman Theatre, Chapter and in the West End. He received the Welsh Theatre Critics Best Actor Award for his performance in *Diary of a Madman* funded by Arts Council Wales, and has toured to India in November 2017 as part of Wales in India, funded by the British Council and Wales Arts International.

### Design / Assistant Producer – Deryn Tudor

During Deryn's time in the industry she has fulfilled many roles within the design and costume field of theatre. She has worked with a variety of theatre companies including Sherman Theatre, Shared Experience, Theatre Centre, Hide Productions, Theatr Y Byd, Theatr Na Nog, Music Theatre Wales, Theatre Iolo, National Theatre Wales, Riverside Theatre, Theatr Genedlaethol Caernarfon, Wales Theatre Company, Theatr Pena, National Dance Company Wales, Living Pictures, has worked on Hairspray Tour UK and was a member of the original production of the West End show *Captain Corelli's Mandolin*.

### Lighting Design – Chris Illingworth

Chris is a highly regarded lighting designer. His works include Ballet Cymru's award-winning production of *Romeo and Juliet* and Theatr Y Byd's *Inside Out* for which he was voted Lighting Designer of the Year. He has designed for Sherman Theatre, Made in Wales and Ransack Dance.

### Production Stage Manager – Gareth Williams

Gareth has worked professionally in the creative industry for 10 years. He has been Technical Stage Manager at the WMC and Sherman Theatre and has worked professionally with NYOW, RWCMD, NTW and as a multi-skilled creative professional in the entertainment industry.

### Thanks to:

Sarah & Mabli, Gilly Adams, David Britton, Nick Davies, Julia Barry, Ruth Till, Kaite O'Reilly, Phillip Zarrilli, Elen & Dylan Bowman, John Campbell, Josie Smith, Helen Prior, DAC, ACW, Julie Morgan, Maggie Dunning, Pete Gregory & Unlimited

### Photo Credit

Photographs provided by John Campbell / roomoflight.com

Cyngor Celfyddydau Cymru
Arts Council of Wales

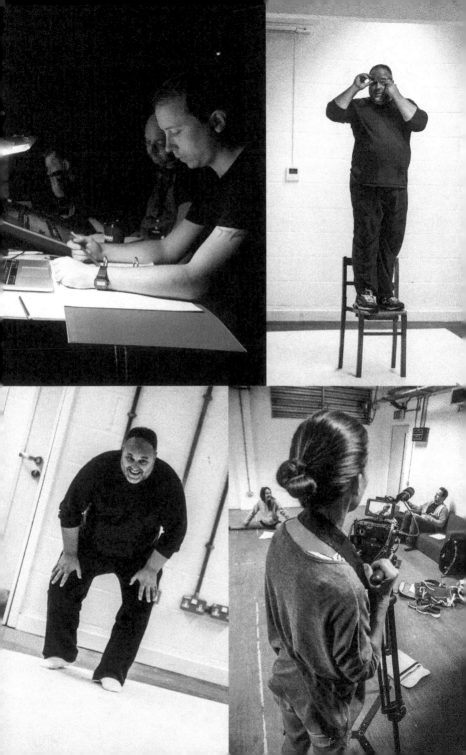

# GODS
# & KINGS

by Paul Whittaker

# ST. CADOC'S HOSPITAL

Community and Mental Health Unit

CAERLEON, GWENT NP6 1XO
TELEPHONE: (0633) 421121   FAX: (0633) 430184

OUTPATIENT CLINIC
COMMUNITY MENTAL HEALTH UNIT
12 PARK SQUARE
NEWPORT
GWENT

Dear  Mr Whittaker

An appointment has been made for you to see Dr Jennie Davies on

Thursday ......19.1.95................... at ...10.15......am
           23.2.95                              10.00   am.
at the Community Mental Health Unit, 12 Park Square, Newport, Gwent
(map enclosed).

If you cannot keep this appointment, please contact me on the above
number, extension 234.

If this is your first appointment, please bring a close relative.

Yours sincerely

Carol Harvey (Mrs)
Secretary to Dr Jennie Davies
Consultant Psychiatrist

21

It's not much to look at, is it?

A simple pill much like any other... but it is so much more. This one was made of metal and if I took it, it would change my life forever.

I wonder if the people who sat in this chair before me felt it was their choice or were they forced into it against their will?

It hasn't been easy, I'll have you know. Since I fled the village I've relocated, without gifts or goodbyes, on more than one occasion. I roamed for thousands of miles and wore out many pairs of shoes. I even sectioned myself in a rural outpost of France because I thought I could escape... but no matter how far I ran every road led me to here.

Relationships, jobs, a name of any kind are hard to maintain on the lam but I knew from a young age that these things aren't meant for me and my kind.

I was so tired. Tired of the running. Tired of being on constant alert, one eye open, fearful that they would break down my door and spirit me away. But I was done with living like an outlaw. I wanted a bed of my own. So reluctantly I turned myself in to them in one of the few places my existence made sense; Newport, South Wales.

The professional face before me gives me a benign smile as I look down at the photocopied document that was so cautiously placed into my outstretched hand, "Welcome to Manic Depression" and so begins my life as a Mental Patient.

As I thumb through the welcome pack I realise that my newfound status is undeserving of colour. Maybe it's too much stimulus. The room is beige, as is my Psychiatrist, Dr Jenny Davies, and the furniture is brown. It is as if the whole setup has been engineered just to keep me calm, which I find immensely irritating.

As I flick through to the lifestyle section of the guide, something else leaps out at me. It's a small section that boldly informs me that manic depression is considered to be a creative disease and that many famous artists and entertainers have suffered from it. Spike Milligan was one, Carrie Fisher was another; and last but not least was dear old Ronnie Scott.

"I think you might want to update this" I inform Jenny.

"Why's that?"

"Ronnie Scott killed himself two weeks ago."

I enjoy watching Dr Davies curse under her breath. I imagine that she is exasperated that such an oversight has occurred. But she is probably just cursing the fact that there are boxes of these corner-stapled anathemas under her desk, scraping at her shins; a constant reminder of the scale of her task.

I feel bad for her, so I do what I always do. I smile to let her know it's okay, to let her know that these things happen, that if you can't laugh at life's misfortunes then surely they will kill you. That is the exact moment she tells me that unless I agree to take lithium I will be dead by the time I am thirty.

Dr Davies, I surmise, needs to work more on her comic timing.

Lithium, for those of you who do not know, is a naturally occurring alkali metal that can be found mainly in the mentally ill and batteries. The singer Kurt Cobain famously penned a track on his *Nevermind* album dedicated to the substance which, as he later put a shotgun in his mouth, was an ode to its medicinal properties, not its ability to both store and release electricity to a wide variety of devices.

The side effects of this wonder-drug include:

**ACNE  BAD TASTE IN THE MOUTH
BALANCE OR COORDINATION PROBLEMS
COMA  CONFUSION  CONVULSIONS
DIABETES  DIARRHOEA  DRY  MOUTH
HAIR LOSS  HEART  PROBLEMS
INCREASED BLOOD SUGAR LEVELS
ITCHING  KIDNEY PROBLEMS
LOSS OF APPETITE  MEMORY PROBLEMS
MUSCLE TWITCHING  NAUSEA
REFLEX PROBLEMS SEXUAL DYSFUNCTION
SPEECH PROBLEMS  STUPOR  THIRST
TREMORS  VERTIGO**

What kind of cure lists coma as a side effect?

Maybe I am sicker than I thought.

To my surprise our appointment is over. No men in white coats lead me to a room with mattressed walls. They don't ask why no one has come with me. They don't even remove my shoelaces or belt. Within twenty minutes of being told that I am not the man on my Student I.D., I am back on the streets with only my user manual for guidance.

What are they thinking?

I sold myself out to be cured not curated. So what am I now? Am I a patient? Every mental I'd read about had killed, so why had they let me go outside? Did Hungerford and Dunblane mean nothing to these people? I was expecting at least a badge or maybe a bell but all they gave me was a handout and three weeks in which to decide my fate.

**Bastards.**

The whole point of giving in was so I didn't have to think any more. Well at least they had given me a diagnosis. That had to mean something, didn't it?

Identity is a strange concept isn't it? Especially when you apply it to a child. You are a son, you are a brother and you are expected to be friends with a cluster of children for sixteen years just because they happen to be born in the same catchment area as you.

"But I don't want to go on holiday with Richard."

"You'll have fun when you get there."

"No I won't. I hate him. He touched his sister's boob."

"Why do you always tell such horrible lies?"

When you are a child, adults are all-powerful. You can't question what they say, and if you disagree with them you are wrong. I understood this by the time I was five years old and knew that photograph wasn't spelt with an 'F'. I was paraded around the school by my teacher to show everyone how clever I was and it was the first time someone had called me *special*.

After a week, my teacher's use of the word *special* also meant precocious and cocky and rude and the truth is I was all of those things but so much more. As I grew older and rose above their challenges, things only got worse. I no longer just felt different. I was different and others had noticed it too.

I used to search for the answers in books. We owned them by the score, shelves upon shelves, piles upon piles, all swept up by the table-load at the end of every jumble sale because we couldn't afford to buy new ones and were banned from the library.

There were books in the school library as well, a quiet world where they sent me when my behaviour was too erratic for class. I read the stories of King Arthur there; as well as those of Odin and Zeus. Gods and kings whose role it was to fight for honour and to protect the weak, the kind of men who wouldn't be scared to challenge David Jupp to be milk monitor and overthrow his break-time tyranny; except, of course, for Zeus who just murdered anyone who got in his way. Apparently Zeus, more than any other god, suffered from the severest of mood swings.

I also met a man called God there. Not *a* god but *the* God. I had found the other gods on the shelf marked 'fiction'. The book of God I found was on the shelf marked 'fact'.

God was everywhere and he saw everything. He saw if you were good. He saw if you were bad. Sometimes the pressure of his judgemental gaze was so great I would hide beneath my bed or travel deep into the countryside to lie beneath a bush for hours on end. Those moments of isolation were my happiest childhood memories – I touched a rabbit once – but deep down I knew I was lying to myself.

**I was never alone. God was everywhere.**

One day after school I was so angry with him for spying on me that I stripped off my uniform, lay on my back and tucked my knees under my chin like a roast chicken so he had to look at my bum hole because it was the worst thing I could think to do.

**God                        didn't                        blink.**

So I used to hide. I used to hide a lot. Despite my fear of heights I would often climb trees and watch the world pass me by. How did they do it? How did they go about their lives knowing that they could be smited at any moment? Of course, now I have my manual I realise that not everyone else thought they were going to die. That was just me. I was such a coward. God, I hated myself. I was even too scared to go to the shops in case they made my heart burst inside my chest and if I did, I zig-zagged down the road to make sure that no one could get within touching distance of me. Not the giant who tipped over the ice cream van on Nomansland Common or Mrs Onions whose bunions forced her to wear slippers like a tweed ninja.

**Dick!**

When I was fourteen I started to imagine I was adopted. That was around the time I became obsessed with being stabbed as I saved the life of an innocent. Gods and kings laid down their lives for what was right. It was their duty and therefore it was mine. It didn't have to be a stabbing; immolation, being shot or crushed by a giant pillar were all viable options but not drowning.

The thought of drowning terrifies me.

That was also the period that I started to hang out with other people's parents. I would pretend to visit a classmate but in truth I was trying to find a home. There were several times I thought I'd found it but there would always be a moment when things turned sour. A racist comment; a misunderstanding of the rules of monopoly and them not understanding that Cilla Black was a bucktoothed demon that heralded the end of all humanity. These were all deal-breakers for me.

Once I'd exhausted all the families I knew, I had no choice but to explore the ones I didn't.

I would slip out of the house under the cover of darkness and patrol the village dressed in black. I would stand in back gardens and watch families as if their windows were rock pools and sometimes, if they were away, I would find an unlocked door or window and climb inside. I never took anything; I never touched their stuff or went through their drawers. I just wanted to see what it felt like to live there...

# I don't want to lie to you.

## Sometimes they were at home.

I also developed other behaviours designed to get people to notice my plight, because if they realised I was different then they would be able to tell me what I was. I would take stupid risks with my safety, I would move in the opposite direction of any trend, and once I cut myself with my pocket knife and submitted my maths homework covered in blood. When I got it back the blood was circled in red pen with the words "what's this?" and an A minus.

By the time I was nineteen years old I had burned so many bridges I had to leave the village.

This is the reason that I welcome my diagnosis with open arms. Bipolar manic depression. It has a nice ring to it and most importantly it makes sense. It makes sense of why I never fitted in. It makes sense of why I came to Newport to do a film degree and it makes me feel like I now have a chance to finally be who I am destined to be. When I tell my friend, Hostel-Girl, of my prognosis on the steps of Barclays Bank she promptly bursts into tears.

"But this is a good thing," I tell her. "Now I know what's wrong with me."

"But there's nothing wrong with you. You're Porl."

Her exotic Scunthorpe drawl always makes my name seem much more interesting than its humble four letters and her teary reaction to my news is a setback, but after we hug for a bit she feels better and says she is away to call her mum because she is a social worker.

The lads of the house simply ask if I am going to get any good drugs.

"THEY SAID I SHOULD TAKE LITHIUM"

"AIN'T THAT IN BATTERIES?"

"Yeah."

"Do you think it'll get you proper fucked up?"

I have no answer to that question. I have no answer to any of their questions.

"Can you still vote?"

"Can you get away with murder?"

"Is that why you act like a dick sometimes?"


This last question is asked by my Welsh-speaking friend, Dyslexic-In-Two-Languages, as he tries to break his own record on the Megadrive. It gets me thinking. Is my illness why I act like a dick sometimes? Is it the reason I do anything? It seemed so straightforward in the beige room. Take the medicine and get better, isn't that what everyone wants? But what if it isn't that simple? My 'condition' has been with me since birth and grew wild and unfettered for nearly a quarter of a century. What if what I think of as my illness is actually me and everything I like about myself is merely a symptom? Maybe there is still something worth fighting for?

As with most big problems we faced as second year arts students we convened the council in front of the condemned gas fire – Hostel Girl, Dyslexic-In-Two-Languages, Dead Dad, and the Unconstructed Male; four displaced souls that made me feel at home. Emulating the oracles of my ancestors we proceed to get stoned off our tits. Once we are in the right frame of mind we decide to create a 'keep & discard' pile of my personality traits.

"How about being the first to dance?"

"He looks well gay when he dances."

"So? That doesn't mean he shouldn't keep it."

"You should definitely keep that thing you do when you just stare at people and freak them out. That's good for Town"

By morning we have drawn up a contract on the back of a roached flyer listing what I am not prepared to lose of myself and if I do, that they have my permission to rescue me by force from the lethal grip of the drugs. To celebrate this historical accord we pack the bong with the remains of the mix and smoke until we all experience dry mouth and eventual stupor, except for Hostel-Girl who has fallen asleep with her darkly furrowed, northern head in my lap. Apparently the hour-long talk she had with her mother has not reassured her about my future one little bit.

From the moment my diagnosis was handed down it never occurred to me that it was something that I might want to keep secret. Why would I? I've quested for answers for years and I am not ashamed of those I have found. In fact, I firmly believe that by being honest with people about who I am my life will become infinitely easier.

"Yeah, you know that time I came into your Post Office, queued for twenty minutes then forgot how to speak? Well it turns out I was being mental.

"And you know that time I came into your supermarket and had that little lie down until you kicked me out? Mental.

"And you know that time I attended your Emergency Room because I set fire to my hand and told you I wasn't a welder and that I had done it to see if my hand was resistant to flames? You wouldn't believe it, I was being a mental not a welder like you wrote in your notes, you fucking idiot."

Also I am not sure where I stand legally. The welcome pack doesn't really cover the topic in much detail, although it does provide me with a short poem about surviving depression. The one thing I am certain of though is that, considering how I have struggled for my first twenty-three years, a policy of honesty cannot possibly cause me any more problems than I already have.

What I haven't considered is that just as my diagnosis has defined me in my eyes, it also re-defines me in the eyes of others. Before I was eccentric but now I am mental.

But
nobody
knew
I
might
be
a
god.

People ask me why I risk my life for others when I can just not get involved. I tell them that it isn't a choice and that I have nothing to lose. Also I never need to be asked. I see something and I act even if that help is undesired like the time I unleashed my simian rage upon a boy for defaming his ex-girlfriend or offered to cut off my finger and send it to UCAS to strengthen a classmate's application. It seemed only reasonable that my severed digit would be worth as much as the two Cs and a D that they were pushing for and that she feared she could not achieve.

This is the reason that I declare war on my degree course but unlike my predecessors I do not swing a sword or throw spears of lightening; I use reason. Logic is my Kung Fu and I can bend it to my will.

Perhaps I am Loki.

I am never angry, I never swear and I never make threats. I am far more irritating than that. I am logical and self-sacrificing, which we all know in an argument is tantamount to cheating. I complete my work and then complain about the lack of equipment, I attend every lecture, even when I am drunk, before I savage its content and when they tell me that unless I cease my campaign for change I will fail the studentship part of my grade and threaten me with failure, I say fail me if you dare.

I

    **AM**

        **BULLET-PROOF**

            **AND THEY**
            **WILL NEVER**
            **SILENCE MY VOICE.**

I

    **SIT**

        **ASTRIDE A**
        **MAGNIFICENTLY**
        **HIGH HORSE**

            **AND THEY**
            **WILL BEND**
            **TO MY WILL.**

There is another reason I push so hard against the controllers of free thought; my put-upon tutor is my ally. It was she that recognised something in me that needed further exploration. Whilst others revelled in my insane behaviour or turned away in fear, she was the one who took me to one side and told me what she saw; a young man in crisis.

"I think you should go and see a Doctor"

"Why? I can beat this"

"I've seen it in my family. You should ask for help."

"I've tried."

I have tried. Smearing blood on my maths homework, setting fire to myself, throwing myself in front of cars, casual alcohol abuse, walking out of a party, hoping that a sensitive soul would notice me like a cheap soap opera. None of it worked and I stopped trying because I had tried everything.

"Have you just tried telling someone?"

What the fuck is she talking about? You can't just tell someone. That's cheating. Arthur pulled a sword, Thor drank so much mead he lowered an ocean and Zeus outwitted his father as he tried to eat him. So how could mine be 'help me'? I need people to realise I am special. But no one ever does because they don't know what special looks like anymore.

I had no choice. I had to take the coward's way out. So I made an appointment with the campus GP and when he asked me what the problem was I told him I wasn't sleeping. He told me not to worry about it because a lot of students took a while to adjust to their new surroundings.

I told him that sometimes I hurt myself, to which he suggested that I moderate my drinking.

Out of sheer desperation I pulled off my sock and showed him my scaly toes. He dismissively informed me it was athlete's foot and signalled that the appointment was over.

As I walked towards the door I took one last shot at redemption.

"I am Jesus and I am hiding because if people find out they will crucify me."

I was sitting in Dr Jenny Davies's office within a week.

An hour later I was breaking the news to my esteemed course leader, a balding peacock of a man who has a history of moving inanimate works of art around galleries. For this reason I am not a supporter of his befuddled regime and, in the spirit of full disclosure, I may show that by being a bit of a dick.

As a visitor to your world it has always amazed me how much resentment, injustice and despair you humans will endure without action. From the very first week of our freshly minted degree course the canteen was alive with the sound of discontent. Everybody agrees that something has to be done but who will heed this rallying cry? Arthur? Odin? Zeus?

Apparently they are unavailable so it has to be me.

My fantasy of dying a hero's death has long since passed. When someone did eventually pull a knife on me, my instinct was to take it off them and not just let them put it in me. But my impulse to stand up to a perceived injustice is overwhelming. I may no longer want to die but I am more than happy to 'sacrifice' myself for the cause. In a previous life I would have tasted the berries or tested the ice. I would be the one to step forth and greet our foe with open eyes and closed fists. I would face the terror in the night. Why, if it wasn't for me, the boys at my high school would never have won the right to wear white socks. I am a relentless warrior and I will make a stand at a drop of a hat unless, of course, that stand is for my benefit – because that would be selfish and egocentric, two things my teacher punished me for in my second year of infant school.

"Oh, I am sorry. I suppose that means you will be leaving."

For the first time in our attritional war our 'glorious' leader has landed a blow that renders me speechless. This is not how I imagined it would go. In my mind I knock politely on his door, tell him I have a mental illness and retire. I never expected that he would interpret these words as my withdrawal from the field of battle. Can he even do that? Have I misplayed my hand? Maybe mentals aren't allowed to attend University. Maybe it is bigger than that, maybe I am not allowed to be around people at all.

"I wasn't leaving."

"But this is going to be tough for you. You should go home and focus on getting better."

"I don't have a home. Why can't I stay?"

"Fine. Stay on the course but don't come in any more. You can get your assignments and turn them in but you are excused from being in attendance."

If that shit had said that to anyone else – I would have scorched the Earth and argued that man out of his job by morning, but as those words are aimed squarely at me I simply say,

"Okay."

"Miss, can I go to the toilet please?"

"You should have gone at break time."

"I didn't need to go then."

"Well you'll have to wait until we've done this."

As I stood cross-legged and watched as my teacher pulled all the twine from our string paintings like an end of pier magician I wet myself.

"Why didn't you tell me you needed to go?"

"I did."

"You didn't tell me you were going to wet yourself."

"You said I couldn't go."

"But I didn't expect you to just stand there and wet yourself. You should have just gone."

"You told me I couldn't."

As I washed my legs in the toilet sink and changed into a set of spare clothes from the 'wet box' I realised I have learned a valuable lesson.

Even though you are told to obey your elders from the day you are born sometimes you have to break the rules. Sometimes, regardless of your disproportionate fear of divine retribution, you simply have to do what you need to do to survive and deal with the consequences later.

It is the first of many Damascene moments and the scales fall from my eyes.

So despite my epic loss to a man in a collarless shirt I take solace in the fact that I manage to walk out in dry underwear, which means that to all those who need to believe in me there is no outward sign of my defeat. After all, I have a reputation to maintain. I am their mental warrior. I never back down and I am the man that knows you need more enemies than friends because your enemies remind you of what needs to be done.

Back in my saddle I head down the staircase towards my tutor's office and my spirits rise – and thanks to the rocket fuel of mania I reach my tutor-slash-saviour's door with my self-belief fully restored and convinced that being excluded from the building was part of my master plan.

"You look tired."

Well at least she is honest.

"What is it?"

"Bipolar manic depression."

"Have they offered you lithium?"

"Yeah."

"Are you going to take it?"

"I just wanted to ask if we can move our tutorial."

"Aren't you feeling well?"

"No I'm fine. I just have to go for an emergency brain scan. They think all the blackouts might be because I have a brain tumour. I can be back by two."

"What?"

"I have to have a brain scan."

 "Then don't come back."

Why would she say that to me? She is supposed to be on my side.

"It's only a brain scan."

"Is anyone going with you?"

"No. I'll catch the bus. So can we move my tutorial or not?"

I can tell she has more thoughts but this is not our first dance. So it is with a great deal of reluctance that she eventually agrees. Despite her acquiescence I can't help but feel let down by her reaction. She's seen me blackout loads of times. In fact, the day she told me to get help I woke up on the floor of her office with a bruise above my eye where I'd hit her desk on the way down.

But she knows me. Blacking out is just how I rest. I can go days without food or sleep and every now and then it catches up with me but after a quick blackout I'm always good to go. She was the one who pushed me into a diagnosis in the first place so why is she suddenly acting like I am someone that needs wrapping in cotton wool? What the hell is everyone's problem with me all of a sudden? I haven't changed.

# WHAT THE FUCK

# IS EVE PRO

# RYONE'S
# BLEM?

Anger drives me onto the bus. I don't like the emotion but I use it. Over the years it has allowed me to achieve amazing things, but it is a power that is filled with darkness that always leaves me with feelings of remorse and shame.

I am three years old. I am sitting on the round rug I know is a whirlpool to another world and I am alone. Except for Kwala. Kwala is a life-sized Koala bear, a gift from an unknown Australian relative who is obviously a big fan of taxidermy. He has a plastic nose and claws but his fur is real and he smells of a musty death. There is a key in his belly that plays Waltzing Matilda when you turn it.

I don't know why it happens. I know it is sunny but I can't recall the trigger. All I know is I have Kwala's ear in my mouth and I am trying to rip it off. I pull so hard I feel a surge of pleasure in my teeth. I grip him tight with both my arms and my legs and I strain my neck back. I smell the colour red.

It only lasts for a moment.

I feel like I have done the worst thing.

As I look down at poor Kwala I see where his ear has begun to separate from the rest of his exposed leathery skin. I feel the taste of his fur in my mouth and I cry.

By the time I reach St Cadocs my anger is gone. I look at the appointment letter in my hand and know that this is the place. It is a strange feeling. In my first year of university I chose to live in halls and fate gave me a room in the building known as Camelot. It was actually part of my address and in week two I met a man called Merlin on the floor below and I knew I had been brought to Newport for a reason. How else you could explain that I was shadowing the life of one of the heroes I'd met on the bookshelves in the quiet room?

Also, what were the chances that opposite the main entrance to the campus stood the red brick walls and municipal green fences of a Psychiatric Hospital? St Cadocs.

My groin tightens. I really don't want to be here but like Orpheus before me I enter Hades and pray that my devil's charm will ensure my passage home.

The first thing I notice is that the place doesn't have what I can easily recognise as an entrance. A tarmac road lures me through the gates but then appears to lead me nowhere. There are sweeping lawns and sprawling buildings but they all have their backs to me. There are no signs and the sounds of the world are strangely muted. What is this place? It is too bright for Hades; too cold for Hell. Is this Avalon? Helheim? Where am I meant to descend and how do I let them know that it is not forever?

I have a letter in my hand and a potential tumour in my head so I push on. Eventually I find a door and a buzzer. I press it. A garbled voice asks me who I am; it hardly challenges the Sphinx for complexity, but still quite a profound question to ask the recently diagnosed. Who am I? I take a punt and read out the name on the appointment letter.

"Paul?"

To my surprise I am right and the door buzzes, shimmies then swings open upon my touch.

I find myself in a dead vestibule bathed in beige twilight. The windows are shrouded in seventies blinds left over from the last time the place was invested in. The white squares of the checkerboard flooring have weathered to a tobacco yellow and the overall lack of colour and contrast makes it hard for me to make out my surroundings. There are over a dozen mismatched chairs but I can't see if the shapes in them are people or shadows. In some cases it proves to be both. A voice calls out to me from a corner that has not yet registered. I turn my head and see a featureless face guide me in from behind a desk. This place makes no sense. Why would they hide the receptionist and why doesn't it look like a hospital? This is more like an institution.

"Are you Paul?" the dappled, faceless drone asks me. She reminds me of the Clay People from the Flash Gordon serials my dad shared with me on Saturday mornings. I check the appointment letter again,

"Yes?"

Ever since my diagnosis that name has started to slip away from me and it is becoming a meaningless sound in my mouth.

| **PAUL.** | **PAWL.** | **PUH.** |
|-----------|-----------|----------|
| **PAUL.** | **PAWL.** | **PUH.** |
| PAUL. | PAWL. | PUH. |
| PAUL. | PAWL. | PUH. |
| PAUL. | PAWL. | PUH. |
| PAUL. | PAWL. | PUH. |
| PAUL. | PAWL. | PUH. |

"They won't be long. Just take a seat."

I take the seat of my choosing with a degree of nonchalance that lets everyone know that I am not a patient. I am simply someone who needs a quick brain scan then I will be returning to my business.

As I sink into the tall-backed leather chair I realise its resistance has long since been broken by the hundreds of buttocks that have occupied it before me and its yielding touch is seductive.

This is also the moment I realise that I am not alone. Two of the shadows are indeed people and a third rattles through a set of doors, his skeletal arms doing just enough to give his wheelchair propulsion. Two thoughts go through my mind: "So this is what mad people look like". And: "Why are they looking at me?"

"Alright?" Shadow One grunts.

"Yes, thanks." I respond.

"You know once you're in this place they never let you out?"

"Never let you out." Shadow Two echoes.

Across the room Shadow Three is wheeling himself bodily against the door to the world beyond but it opens inwards against his legs, causing himself to be the obstacle to his own freedom. As he rolls back to allow the door to open, the handle slips from his feeble grasp and it swings closed. With a Sisyphean resolve he rolls forward once more. As the door opens into his legs I look away.

"The thing is they never let you out."

"Paul? They are ready for you now."

I hum their siren song from my ears. I am not going to fall under their spell because I am not one of them. I have a life to lead, a bed to sleep in and the desperate need to be elsewhere. I turn and the Clay Person points towards a corridor. I head for it and leave my welcome party to their mutterings.

A young man awaits me in a doorway. In his mind he probably sees himself as a healer but I know a technician when I see one. He is just here to wire me to the machine.

"Take a seat."

It occurs to me that I am less than two days into my diagnosis and there have been a lot of chair-based activities. Maybe they know my feet are made of clay. I take the seat and it tilts back just far enough to make it feel like science. As he places the strangely wired headset over my snakelike hair he casually asks,

"Are you on any drugs?"

"Not at the moment."

"Good, because the guy in here before you was tripping and he flipped out."

"What are you doing exactly?"

"An EEG."

"And that will tell you if I have a tumour?"

"No, this is for epilepsy."

"They said I was being checked for a tumour."

"Not by me. You'll have to go somewhere else for that. There you go."

With a final tweak of my head-wires he satisfies himself that I am tethered correctly. I have seen the device on the trolley in movies. Why have they strapped me to a lie detector? What are they going to ask me? I look on in fascination as the paper scrolls and the needles scribble like hungry elves.

"Paul?"

"Yes."

The machine whirrs into life and scratches my thoughts onto the page.

"I'm going to place a strobe light in front of you and run it to see if we can trigger a seizure."

"Okay."

The machine scribbles again. I am seeing my own thoughts. Now I know what my words look like in their purest form. Maybe this machine can tell me who I am. But alas my view of it is blocked as he swings the strobe light into my field of vision. It is surprisingly big.

"Now I'm going to start low and then slowly increase the frequency."

"Okay."

**Scribble.**           **Scribble.**                **Scribble.**

The strobe's godly flicker fills my world and before long I stop staring at it and start swimming in it. This is amazing. I leave my chair behind and look down upon myself. The cap and wires morph into snakes striking at the sky. Away to the right the needles have become fists gripping crayons angrily scrawling my thoughts onto a roll of wallpaper that gathers in a bin.

**THEN I SEE THE EVENT HORIZON;**

**FLY THROUGH IT AND ORGANISE**

**THE CHAOS OF THE UNIVERSE**

**INTO CALM:**

**I AM A FIXED POINT**

**IN THE UNIVERSE**

**AND IT REVOLVES AROUND ME:**

"Okay. The machine says you haven't got epilepsy."

But not whether I have a tumour or not.

The next week and half passes by in my regular routine of seeking out normalcy with the clean-living Day Folk to keep me occupied. Then I move onto the Twilight People, whose nights are done by midnight, and finally I return to the Nocturnals in my flat, where we smoke and drink until dawn and we fall into our pits. After around an hour of coma I rise from the dead and re-join the Day Folk in their wholesome endeavours just like a real boy, and do it all over again.

The appointment letter for the brain scan has yet to materialise because, as it turns out, a potential brain tumour is not an emergency procedure, but I do not care. I am confident that it does not exist. I will play their game and submit myself to their magnetic imaging technology but it would be all too convenient for them to be able to look at the riddle of me and say,

"The answer lies here. If we remove it he will be normal."

I understand that the world needs explanations and definitions. It is appalled by mystery because mystery makes it feel powerless and small. But I also understand that Psychiatry is not a Science. It is an art open to interpretation and misuse. Line up any two people with the same mental condition and you will find just as many differences as similarities. We are simply placed in categories to aid in our classification and drug regimens. Apparently I am only two slight tweaks away from being schizophrenic.

Then my brain scan would be an emergency.

I have decided to take the lithium. I had convinced myself that it isn't worth the risk but my brief sojourn to the Island of the Institutionalised and my time with its Shadow Beings has convinced me otherwise. What if they are my future? What if they too had chosen to refuse to play the game? Those men are neither gods nor kings, they are merely wastrels locked in labyrinthine minds, their golden thread to reality long since fallen from their grasp. A place from which, as Shadow Two echoed,

"They never let you out."

On opting to take the pills I also make the decision to abide by its many complex rules.

Lithium, it turns out, is not a party-loving drug. It is the puritan of pills. It eschews such vices as alcohol, cola, coffee, saturated fats and carbohydrates. This means that as a roommate lithium is a bit of a dick but, as my friends often remind me, so am I – so who am I to judge?

I also feel it is important to ritualise the taking of the first pill and shift its intended start date a few days so it coincides with my twenty-third birthday, at which of course I will now have to forego the shots and sausage rolls, because lithium will be upset and boil my blood – the dick. It is easily arranged. Meet at ours after the pub, bring what you need, make sure there are more Rizla than cigarettes and any blood spilt has to be mine.

As I stand in my living room, pill nestled in my palm, I am surrounded by as many people who wish me ill than care for me, which means at least fifty percent of them are going to be happy with the outcome. I look at the pill, which I know is white but I always see as a minty green, and then I look at the ragtag people I have gathered closest to me. Hostel Girl, Dyslexic-in-Two-Languages, Dead Dad and the Unconstructed-Male. They have even chipped in and bought me a pill box to keep my medication in. They watch in awe as I raise it to my lips. I swallow it down with a slug of water and wait.

**Nothing.**                    **Nothing happens at all.**

I can sense their disappointment.

"Apparently it takes three months to get into your system."
I tell them.

And so as the party rages around me I wait because I know
something else that I haven't told them. I haven't taken it yet.

I have always known I am a god or a king. What I don't know
is which one I am because my soul is split in two.

I can only preach peace because I am capable of war.

I enjoy the role of predator as much as I embrace the role of
shepherd.

Light and dark.

My two opposing sides keep me in balance but now that
balance is about to be upset and this pill is going to determine
who I am to be.  I just hope that when it is done with me I
still know who I am.

# He takes
# the pill.

# Curtain.

Gwent Community Health
National Health Service Trust
12 Park Square
Newport
Gwent, NP9 4EL
Tel (Switch Board) 0633 263388

Iechyd Cymuned Gwent
Ymddiriedolaeth Gwasanaeth Iechyd Gwladol
12 Park Square
Casnewydd
Gwent, NP9 4EL
Rhif ffôn (Switsfwrdd) 0633 263388

Our Ref: OP/BJ/LITHIUM
Ext: 219

## LITHIUM CLINIC

21.3.95

Dear *Mr Whittaker,*

An appointment has been made for you to attend the Lithium Clinic
on *Monday 3rd April* ............. at *10 Am* ............

**THESE TESTS ARE IMPORTANT**, therefore, if you are unable to
attend, could you please telephone us on the above number, so
that an alternative appointment can be made.

Please bring a list of any medication you are taking.

Yours sincerely

*Olive Priddis*

**OLIVE PRIDDIS**
**Staff Nurse**

# Additional

# Materials

# A Note on these Resources

When Paul wrote *Gods & Kings* as part of his MA, he did so with the confidence that only his tutor and his seven classmates were ever going to read it. After completing the module successfully, the essay sat on his desk for weeks waiting to be filed away in a drawer. Then two things happened that changed everything.

Robert Bowman picked it up and asked if he could borrow it, so that he had something to read on the train. By the end of the train journey he had sent Paul a text asking if he could perform it.

At the same time, Paul showed it to PhD student Nicole Burchett. After reading *Gods & Kings*, Nicole saw an alternative use for the play and asked if she could use it as a basis for a lecture she had to deliver to psychology undergraduates on the 'consequences of receiving a mental health diagnosis.'

It was those two unrelated events that inextricably linked the arts and health aspects of Paul's story, and gave credence to the notion that *Gods & Kings* could be transformed from a private revelation into a public performance.

**Paul:** The reason I brought Tamsin on to the project early on is because she has a diagnosis as well; if I was going to put my story out there warts and all, it had to be worth something. And the best way to make it worth something was keep it authentic. I knew Tamsin would be able to give me the strength to keep it truthful when my instinct told me to hide the most painful parts of my story.

**Tamsin:** As service users, it was really important to us to ensure that it remained authentic and we didn't theatricalise it to the point where it lost the core of what it was about. And so we worked really hard with Robbie and the team just to make sure that it remained honest, and a story that people can really, truly connect to.

**Paul:** We had brilliant support from ACW and the Sherman Theatre in the development of the work. They were both keen to support our approach but they had valid concerns. Was there an audience for an authentic patient experience? How would you market a story about a man's struggle with his Mental Health without making it sound bleak and depressing?

**Tamsin:** We didn't really know if there would be an audience. We did five performances at the Sherman and on the opening night, we were sat there in the foyer, a bit nervous as I always am on opening night of a show, and we were thinking, "Is anyone going to turn up?" So, we were just sat there, and as people flooded into the Sherman foyer we genuinely asked ourselves "Why are all these people here?" "Is there another show on? I wonder what show it is." There was no other show. They were all there to see *Gods & Kings* and we just laughed at each other.

Over the course of the run people travelled to Cardiff from Swindon, Reading, Swansea and the Valleys because of the subject matter of the play. People were hungry to talk about mental illness. Contrary to the concerns that there would be no audience, in addition to the traditional theatre audiences, it appealed to service users, health and social care professionals, educators, politicians, arts professionals and asylum seekers.

The play received critical acclaim and praise from the health sector, and the production was recognised as Best Practice by Arts Council Wales in its report '*Arts and Health in Wales – A Mapping study of current activity*':

> *Gods & Kings* is an opportunity to hear and experience an authentic perspective on experiencing both mental health issues and accessing services. It is honest, heartfelt and it reminds us of how we, as a service, should value what is important to the people we work with and how that understanding is fundamental to enabling their recovery/discovery.
>
> *Andrea Gray – Mental Health Development Lead for Wales,*
> *1000 Lives Improvement/Improvement Cymru, Public Health Wales*

I was so smacked in the face by the veracity of what I was hearing and seeing that I found it almost unbearable. I wanted to keep joining in, wanting to say YES and say, Jesus, I have felt that, I have seen that – and I have never said a word to anyone about it nor heard another human being say what I had experienced and what I had thought, felt and still think and feel.

*Mike Smith – Arts Scene Wales*

When it came to publishing the play text, we worked with the Oberon team and realised that we had an opportunity to add additional support to both the arts and health sectors, by including materials that explored the link between the play and bipolar manic depression.

Aware that people who share any mental health diagnosis are vastly different, we approached the National Centre of Mental Health for their advice, and seeing the potential in this idea, they donated their research for us to incorporate and adapt to increase people's understanding of bipolar and mental illness in general. What are 'grandiose thoughts'? What does depression feel like to someone who is unaware that they are living with it?

As we read through the research, we realised there was a unique opportunity to use excerpts from the text to illustrate the condition to theatre makers, health professionals, and audiences alike, and to give them an insight of what it is like to live with a chronic mental illness, beyond the functionality of the medical model.

This is how the mental health section of our book came into existence.

**Paul Whittaker & Tamsin Griffiths**
**Four in Four**

## Who are Four In Four?

Tamsin Griffiths and Paul Whittaker are cross disciplinary artists with a mental health (MH) diagnosis, based in Cardiff.

We create participatory interactive projects that blur the boundaries of art-forms and challenge perceptions about MH, through form and content. Working in collaboration, we merge our expertise from the worlds of visual arts, theatre, audio, the written word, film, dance and physical performance.

We are passionate advocates of mental health. Its authentic portrayal though the arts is important to us as we consider it vital to social change and how we talk about it.

The arts are a powerful tool for engagement and conversation, which is why everything we create is considered and represents mental health in its most raw and truest form; with humour, compassion and empathy. We have a 'Duty of Care for All' philosophy that lies at the heart of all our work.

As service users and artists who work in public health, we know how important it is to gather the experiences and thoughts of those with lived experience to underpin our creative output. To this end, our practice follows that of the iterative design process.

Our quality has been recognised by ACW who deemed our theatre production *Gods & Kings* as Best Practice in their *Arts and Health in Wales: A Mapping study of current activity – Volume 1: Analysis, findings and proposals January 2018.*

We sit on numerous advisory panels and work with Public Health Wales and 1000 Lives Improvement to consult on the development of Mental Health services across Wales.

Our clients include: *Public Health Wales, NHS Cymru, Llandough Hospital, Hafan y Coed , Mind Cymru, The National Centre for Mental Health, Welsh Government, ACW, Sherman Theatre, Rubicon Dance, the Schools Service and Universities.*

Material in this section is kindly provided by the National Centre for Mental Health/Bipolar Education Programme Cymru and Four in Four.

# Bipolar disorder

Bipolar disorder is a complex brain disorder in which people experience episodes of low and high mood. NOT a character flaw, a personality defect, or your own fault. Everyone experiences changes in mood from time to time. People with bipolar disorder do not just have severe mood swings but can experience severe episodes of illness.

- ▸ Psychotic symptoms can occur during severe episodes of depression and mania.

- ▸ It's not unusual to get manic-type symptoms during depressive episodes and depressive symptoms during manic episodes. These are called 'mixed episodes'.

- ▸ Anxiety symptoms are extremely common in bipolar disorder.

## Types of bipolar disorder

People with bipolar disorder have episodes of low mood (depression) and episodes of high mood (mania or hypomania). Hypomania is a less severe form of mania.

Everyone with bipolar disorder will experience the condition differently. Some people have lots of episodes (sometimes called rapid-cycling) whereas other people with bipolar disorder can be well for long periods of time.

The terms Bipolar I and Bipolar II are sometimes used to describe two forms of the condition.

People with Bipolar I experience severe episodes of high mood (mania), while people with Bipolar II experience less severe high mood (hypomania). Both will experience episodes of depression.

## Symptoms of bipolar disorder

"Line up any two people with the same mental condition and you will find just as many differences as similarities. We are simply placed in categories to aid in our classification and drug regimens. Apparently I am only two slight tweaks away from being schizophrenic." [pg 53, aged 22]

## Depression

### Feelings

Sad, Low,
Empty,
Hopeless,
Irritable,
Guilty

"I am three years old. I am sitting on the round rug I know is a whirlpool to another world and I am alone. Except for Kwala...

...I don't know why it happens. I know it is sunny but I can't recall the trigger. All I know is I have Kwala's ear in my mouth and I am trying to rip it off. I pull so hard I feel a surge of pleasure in my teeth. I grip him tight with both my arms and my legs and I strain my neck back. I smell the colour red. It only lasts for a moment. I feel like I have done the worst thing.

As I look down at poor Kwala I see where his ear has begun to separate from the rest of his exposed leathery skin. I feel the taste of his fur in my mouth and I cry." [pg 44, aged 3]

### Thoughts

Dulled
thinking

"Yeah, you know that time I came into your Post Office, queued for twenty minutes then forgot how to speak? Well it turns out I was being mental." [pg 33, aged 21]

Poor
concentration

"There were books in the school library as well, a quiet world where they sent me when my behaviour was too erratic for class." [pg28, aged 6]

**Poor memory**

**PW:** Because I was scared the bus driver would kill me it used to take me over half an hour to run to my girlfriend's house. There were no pavements and in the summer the flies used to fly into my mouth or cling to the river of sweat that streamed from my bright red face. One day I arrived at her door with an overwhelming sense of smugness because for the first time I wasn't breathing through a crippling stitch. When she opened the door my smugness was wiped away by the sight of her red swollen eyes and tear-stained cheeks. Suddenly sick to my stomach, I asked her what was wrong and her words fell out of her mouth in a stream of jagged sobs.

"Where – have – you – been? I – thought – you – were – dead"

"Why?"

"Because – your – Mum – said – you – left – two – hours – ago!"

To this day I cannot remember where that time went.

[lived experience aged 14]

**Poor attention**

**PW:** Bastille night was one of the biggest nights of the year for the idyllic Bourg of Bourganeuf. Almost a thousand locals poured into the town from every hamlet, village and farmstead to spend the evening drinking and shouting colours into the air as the fireworks lit up the night sky, terrorising the wildlife for miles around. Desperate to cross the ancient square, I put my head down and wove between the mass of joyful limbs and foreign tongues. I eventually fell into a pocket of calm and found my breath. I had made it – but when I looked up I realised something was desperately wrong. Either side of me there stood a throng of expectant faces, which upon seeing me turned to confusion. The gap I had fallen through had closed behind me and I suddenly realised that I was now leading a forty-strong torch parade. I was unable to get out of its way as we rounded the turret of the town hall and I was swept down the hill. [lived experience, aged 20]

**Worried about minor issues**

"As I thumb through the welcome pack I realise that my newfound status is undeserving of colour. Maybe it's too much stimulus. The room is beige, as is my Psychiatrist, Dr Jenny Davies, and the furniture is brown. It is as if the whole setup has been engineered just to keep me calm, which I find immensely irritating." [pg 23, aged 22]

**Pessimistic**

"Relationships, jobs, a name of any kind are hard to maintain on the lam but I knew from a young age that these things aren't meant for me and my kind. I was so tired. Tired of the running. Tired of being on constant alert, one eye open, fearful that they would break down my door and spirit me away." [pg 23, aged 22]

**Indifference**

"I just wanted to ask if we can move our tutorial."

"Aren't you feeling well?"

"No I'm fine. I just have to go for an emergency brain scan. They think all the blackouts might be because I have a brain tumour. I can be back by two."

"What?"

"I have to have a brain scan."

"Then don't come back."

Why would she say that to me? She is supposed to be on my side.

"It's only a brain scan."

"Is anyone going with you?"

"No. I'll catch the bus. So can we move my tutorial or not?". [pg 40 aged 22]

**Thinking about death and dying**

"Gods and kings laid down their lives for what was right. It was their duty and therefore it was mine. It didn't have to be a stabbing; immolation, being shot or crushed by a giant pillar were all viable options, but not drowning. The thought of drowning terrifies me" [pg 30, aged 22]

**Suicidal**

**PW:** As I stood on the bridge with the rail against my back I looked down into the blackness of the fast flowing water. All I had to do was let go and it would be over. I didn't imagine the fall. I imagined being under the water, its coldness embracing me as I opened my mouth and invited it to flow into my lungs. I would become one with the river and it would carry me away from the heaviness inside my head.

I closed my eyes and let go. But the water didn't swallow me. It wasn't deep enough. Instead, I landed upright with a jarring pain in my knees and a pang of humiliation. Thankful that no one had witnessed my failure I waded to the riverbank and slunk home through the shadows. As I pushed open the front door I could hear my family watching television in the living room. Taking them two at a time, I snuck upstairs and hid my wet trousers under my bed. [lived experience aged 18]

| Psychotic symptoms | I see something and I act, even if that help is undesired. Like the time I unleashed my simian rage upon a boy for defaming his ex-girlfriend, or offered to cut off my finger and send it to UCAS to strengthen a classmate's application. It seemed only reasonable that my severed digit would be worth as much as the two Cs and a D that they were pushing for and that she feared she could not achieve. |

This is the reason that I declare war on my degree course, but unlike my predecessors I do not swing a sword or throw spears of lightening; I use reason. Logic is my kung fu and I can bend it to my will.

Perhaps I am Loki. [pg 34, aged 22]

## Behaviours

| Sleep less /more | "The next week and half passes by in my regular routine of seeking out normalcy with the clean-living Day Folk to keep me occupied. Then I move onto the Twilight People, whose nights are done by midnight, and finally I return to the Nocturnals in my flat, where we smoke and drink until dawn and we fall into our pits. After around an hour of coma I rise from the dead and re-join the Day Folk in their wholesome endeavours just like a real boy, and do it all over again." [pg 53, age 22] |

| | |
|---|---|
| Eat less/more | **PW:** Sometimes it feels like my stomach is being squeezed by a clenched fist that won't let go. I know I have to eat but if I manage to force down more than a mouthful of food it sits in me like a dull rock and pins me down. The longer my depression lasts the harder the fist grips me. I can feel every finger as it pulls tighter and tighter and I begin to imagine that I will never eat again [lived experience 21 years – present day] |
| Less active | **PW:** I loved playing football. I played in a Saturday league, a Sunday league, a five-a-side league and trained for two hours every Wednesday night. One morning I woke up and thought "You can't play today". As I thought I'd want to play the following week I feigned a knee injury and told my teammates I couldn't even be a linesman. The week after that I still couldn't play, even though my teammates kept telling me they needed me. Eventually the pressure of saying no and letting them down was so great I bought a walking stick and used it until people stopped asking me to play. [lived experience aged 17] |
| Easily tired | **PW:** One day I noticed a brown letter from Income Support laying on my doormat, my name and address visible to all through the plastic window. After letting it rest for a couple of days I eventually opened it at arm's length and went back to bed to recover from the effort. The next day I took the letter out of the envelope and discovered that my benefits were going to be stopped unless I supplied them with the information they already had. The next day I found the information they asked for, the day after that |

I put it in an envelope and the day after that I posted it. As I walked back from the post office I felt incredibly proud of the effort I had put in. [lived experience aged 27]

| | |
|---|---|
| Restless | "I used to search for the answers in books. We owned them by the score, shelves upon shelves, piles upon piles, all swept up by the table-load at the end of every jumble sale because we couldn't afford to buy new ones and were banned from the library." [pg 28, aged 8] |
| Apathetic | "If that shit had said that to anyone else – I would have scorched the Earth and argued that man out of his job by morning but as those words are aimed squarely at me I simply say, 'Okay.'" [pg 38 aged 22] |

## Mania

### Feelings

| | |
|---|---|
| High, Happy, Elated, Euphoric, Excited, Irritable, Impatient, 'Over-reactive' to minor events | "In a previous life I would have tasted the berries or tested the ice. I would be the one to step forth and greet our foe with open eyes and closed fists. I would face the terror in the night. Why, if it wasn't for me the boys at my high school would never have won the right to wear white socks." [pg 37, aged 22] |

### Thoughts

| | |
|---|---|
| Racing thoughts | "A voice calls out to me from a corner that has not yet registered. I turn my head and see a featureless face guide me in from behind a desk. This place makes no sense. Why would |

they hide the receptionist and why doesn't it look like a hospital? This is more like an institution." [pg 47, aged 22]

**Grandiose ideas and plans**

"I am bullet-proof and they will never silence my voice. I sit astride a magnificently high horse and they will bend to my will." [pg 35, aged 22]

**More creative**

**PW:** Rocket fuel coursed through my veins. My head was full of bees and every one of them had so many ideas that I struggled to process them all. Luckily I had my own video camera so I constantly made films to relieve the pressure and stop from myself from exploding. After watching me leave another house party to make yet another film a classmate sneered,

'You don't think anything you do matters unless you put it on film.'

But the truth was, if I didn't turn my thoughts into film they would be my reality. [lived experience, aged 22]

**Optimistic**

"From the moment my diagnosis was handed down it never occurred to me that it was something that I might want to keep secret. Why would I? I've quested for answers for years and I am not ashamed of those I have found. In fact, I firmly believe that by being honest with people about who I am my life will become infinitely easier." [pg 33, aged 22]

**Easily distracted**

A young man awaits me in a doorway. In his mind he probably sees himself as a healer but I know a technician when I see one. He is just here to wire me to the machine.

'Take a seat.'"

"It occurs to me that I am less than two days into my diagnosis and there have been a lot of chair-based activities. Maybe they know my feet are made of clay. I take the seat and it tilts back just far enough to make it feel like science." [pg 50, aged 22]

## Behaviours

Over-reactive

"She was the one who pushed me into a diagnosis in the first place so why is she suddenly acting like I am someone that needs wrapping in cotton wool? What the hell is everyone's problem with me all of a sudden? I haven't changed.

What the fuck is everyone's problem?" [pg 41 aged 22]

More talkative

"And you know that time I attended your Emergency Room because I set fire to my hand and told you I wasn't a welder and that I had done it to see if my hand was resistant to flames? You wouldn't believe it, I was being a mental, not a welder like you wrote in your notes, you fucking idiot." [pg 33 aged 22]

More socially active

As with most big problems we faced as second year arts students we convened the council in front of the condemned gas fire – Hostel Girl, Dyslexic-In-Two-Languages, Dead Dad, and the Unconstructed Male; four displaced souls that made me feel at home. Emulating the oracles of my ancestors we proceed to get stoned off our tits. [pg 32 aged 22]

Socially disinhibited

"How about being the first to dance?"

"He looks well gay when he dances."

"So? That doesn't mean he shouldn't keep it."
[pg 32 aged 22]

| | |
|---|---|
| Risky behaviours | "It is easily arranged. Meet at ours after the pub, bring what you need, make sure there are more Rizla than cigarettes and any blood spilt has to be mine." [pg 54 aged 23] |
| Spending too much money | N/A |
| Sexually promiscuous | N/A |
| More productive | "But she knows me. Blacking out is just how I rest. I can go days without food or sleep and every now and then it catches up with me but after a quick blackout I'm always good to go." [pg 41 aged 22] |
| Annoying to others | "As I stand in my living room, pill nestled in my palm, I am surrounded by as many people who wish me ill than care for me, which means at least fifty percent of them are going to be happy with the outcome." [pg 54 aged 23] |
| Argumentative | "I am never angry, I never swear and I never make threats. I am far more irritating than that. I am logical and self-sacrificing, which we all know in an argument is tantamount to cheating. I complete my work and then complain about the lack of equipment, I attend every lecture, even when I am drunk, before I savage its content and when they tell me that unless I cease my campaign for change I will fail the studentship part of my grade and threaten me with failure, I say fail me if you dare." [pg 35 aged 22] |

## Causes of bipolar disorder

- Lots of factors play a role in causing bipolar disorder. There is a strong biological basis but its onset often coincides with a stressful life event.

- Bipolar disorder can be thought of as a malfunctioning "mood-thermostat" in the brain.

- Some people are more vulnerable to bipolar disorder and need less to trigger an episode of illness.

Bipolar disorder is due to a combination of biological, psychological and social factors. Although it has a clear underlying genetic basis it is not caused just by your genes or indeed just by your upbringing or life experiences (see the diagram below).

More research is needed to help us understand the causes of bipolar disorder and how to help people better who experience this condition.

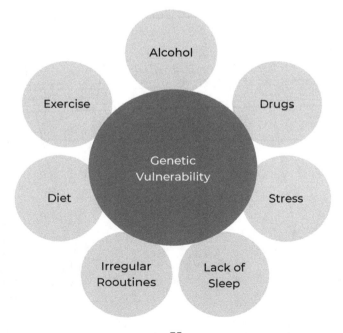

## National Centre for Mental Health

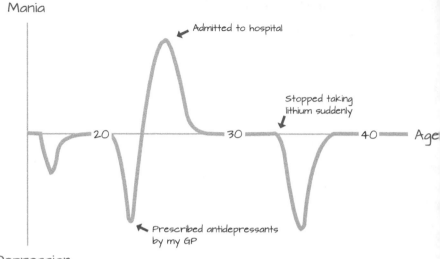

## God's & King's life chart

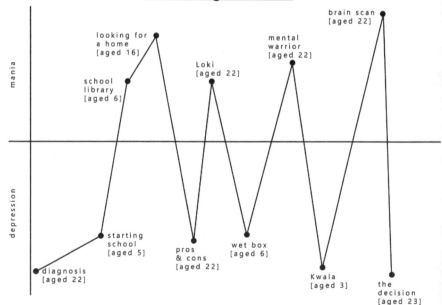

## Pros of taking medication (NCMH)

► I'm getting depressed less often on my medication

► Allows me to socialise

► I get less anxious

► I've got more money because I spend less

► My relatonships are better

► It keeps me out of hospital

► My sleep and concentration are better

## Cons of taking medication

► I think that being on medication can be stigmatising

► I don't like the regular blood tests

► I feel too sedated on some medication I've taken

► I miss my creativity

► I miss the high periods

► I don't like the side affects (weight gain)

## Pros of taking medication (Paul W.)

► I can't live like this anymore

► I should care if I live or die

► I am scaring people that I care about

► I feel like a monster

► I always feel alone

► What happens when I leave university?

► I want someone else to take control of my life

## Paul's cons of taking medication

► My illness makes me invincible

► What if I can't dance anymore?

► Is my sense of humour a symptom?

► The drugs could kill me

► I won't be me anymore

► I like being a God

## Types of medication used in bipolar disorder

**Mood stabilisers** are the key to maintaining stable, even moods.

**Antidepressants** are used to treat bipolar depression but:

- ▸ MAY not work very well for bipolar depression.
- ▸ MAY trigger mania in some people with bipolar disorder.
- ▸ MAY increase mood cycling in some people.

**Antipsychotics are useful in managing psychotic experiences and in treatment of mania (although it does not necessarily mean that you have psychosis if you are prescribed antipsychotics).**

*For more information about bipolar, please visit Bipolar UK:* **https://www.bipolaruk.org**

*For more information on medication, please visit the National Centre for Mental Health:* **https://www.ncmh.info/medication/**

**An Access Guide for venues to support the staff, audience and the Company. Created by Tamsin Griffiths and Paul Whittaker.**

## For Box Office

An email outlining the access provision should be sent out to all audience members, so that those with access needs know that they will be accommodated in advance. This information should also be detailed on the website.

Suggested content for email:

- Please identify yourself at the box office on arrival if you require any support or assistance.

- You can reserve a seat in advance or on arrival. You can request to preview the space in advance of the performance / seat booking to support any additional needs.

- It is possible to enter the theatre up to 30 minutes before the performance starts if required.

- If you leave the theatre during the show, an usher will guide you back to your seat. Please note that it may not be possible to return to your original seat.

- A quiet space is available throughout the evening should you require. The room will be clearly signposted or you can ask an usher to guide you.

- A BSL preshow talk and preview of the space are available prior to the start of the performance. Please speak to a member of box office and they will arrange this for you.

- Should you have any questions prior to the performance then please don't hesitate to contact us.

# Example Box Office email

### *Selecting your seat*

You can pick your seat in advance of your visit, even if we are not using a seating chart to sell the event. You can ask to preview the space, choose your seat and we will make sure that seat is yours when you arrive.

To make an appointment to preview your seat or if you want to discuss anything else about your visit you can phone us on ...................., email us at ............................. or call in and have a chat with our box office team.

We will open the doors of the auditorium 30 minutes before the advertised start time of the performance so if it takes you a bit more time to get comfortable that's absolutely fine.

### *Leaving the Auditorium*

If you leave your seat during the show an usher will guide you out and back in when you are ready. Unfortunately we may not always be able to get you back to your original seat.

If you need a quiet space during the evening we will have one available. It will be clearly signposted but a member of our team will be more than happy to show you the way.

### *Post Show*

A post show panel conversation (with British Sign Language) will take place around five minutes after the show so if you want to leave the auditorium for a comfort break and then re-enter you will be more than welcome to.

Please feel free to get in touch about any aspect of your visit, we are always happy to answer any questions or queries.

We look forward to seeing you soon.

........................ Box Office Team

(the above example was contributed by the Riverfront Box Office Team)

## For Front of House

- Allow audience members to reserve their seat either on booking, on arrival or in advance of performance date (once booked).

- Audience members that have reserved a seat should not be asked to move by a member of staff or ushers.

- Please liaise with the company to provide a pre-show talk for audience members who have requested in advance (BSL).

- Please provide a space and a table to display mental health literature.

- Please provide a dedicated Quiet Space for audience members. The Quiet Space should be clearly signposted and ushers should be made aware of where it is. Plenty of water and glasses should be provided in the quiet space.

- Some audience members may wish to take their seat in the theatre early. We would recommend that the house opens 15 mins earlier than usual, but no more than 30 mins before the performance starts.

- Some audience members may request to see the theatre space earlier than 30 minutes before the performance. Please lialse with the company to arrange this.

- The company will require an alternative space to warm up 30 minutes before each performance.

- If an audience member leaves during the show please check if they are OK or require any assistance – but do not 'over-fuss'. Please let them know that they only need to ask if they need anything and there is a quiet space available should they need it.

- If an audience member leaves the theatre during the performance, an usher should be available to guide them back to their seat. Please note that it may not be possible to return them to their original seat, to keep distractions to a minimum during the performance.

- At the end of the performance, please ask the Front of House Manager to announce that a post-show discussion will start in 10 minutes. Audience members may leave the space and return, or wait in their seats. The post-show discussion should also be accessible to members of the public who did not see the show. Please do a front of house announcement prior to the start of the post-show discussion.

- As some participants may be reluctant to ask a question in person during the post-show discussion, please provide an area where they can submit their questions in written form so they can be read out to the panel by the compère. The panel chair/compère should receive these at the commencement of the discussion.

- The post-show discussion should last a maximum of 45 minutes but can be shorter based on the judgement of the panel chair.

## For the Company

- The house will be open 15 minutes earlier than usual but no more than 30 minutes before the performance starts. Please plan your warm-up accordingly. There will be a warm up space available to use, separate from the theatre should you require.

- Please be aware that audience members may leave the theatre and possibly return throughout the show.

- A member of the company will brief the ushers on:
  - The content of the play
  - The access provided
  - The mental health resources on display
  - The Four in Four Company

- If BSL audience members request a pre-show talk, please liaise with the venue to provide one.

- There will be a 10 minute turnaround between the performance and the post-show discussion.

- The post-show discussion should last a maximum of 45 minutes but can be shorter based on the judgement of the panel Chair.

- Company contact/information details are available on request for those who ask for them, i.e. website, social media platforms.

## Contact Information:

**Website** www.fourinfour.co.uk

**Email** info@fourinfour.co.uk

**Instagram** @FourinFour_ArtsandHealth

**Facebook** Four in Four – Arts & Health / @FourinFourWales

**Twitter** @FourinFour1

WWW.OBERONBOOKS.COM

Follow us on Twitter @oberonbooks
& Facebook @OberonBooksLondon